Joined by Fate

INTERTWINED B

THOMAS
JEFFERSON
AND
SALLY
HEMINGS

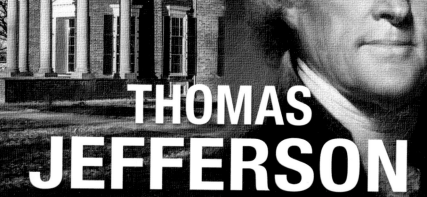

THOMAS JEFFERSON

AND

SALLY HEMINGS

DEL SANDEEN

E Enslow Publishing
101 W. 23rd Street
Suite 240
New York, NY 10011
USA
enslow.com

Published in 2019 by Enslow Publishing, LLC.
101 W. 23rd Street, Suite 240, New York, NY 10011

Library of Congress Cataloging-in-Publication Data

Names: Sandeen, Del, author.
Title: Thomas Jefferson and Sally Hemings / Del Sandeen.
Description: New York : Enslow, 2019. | Series: Joined by fate: Intertwined biographies |
    Includes bibliographical references and index. | Audience: Grades 7–12.
Identifiers: LCCN 2017053841| ISBN 9780766098244 (library bound) |
    ISBN 9780766098251 (pbk.)
Subjects: LCSH: Jefferson, Thomas, 1743–1826—Relations with women—Juvenile
    literature. | Jefferson, Thomas, 1743–1826—Relations with slaves—Juvenile literature.
    | Hemings, Sally—Juvenile literature. | CYAC: Hemings, Sally—Family—Juvenile
    literature.
Classification: LCC E332.2 .S25 2019 | DDC 973.4/60922—dc23
LC record available at https://lccn.loc.gov/2017053841

Printed in the United States of America

To Our Readers: We have done our best to make sure all website addresses in this book
were active and appropriate when we went to press. However, the author and the publisher
have no control over and assume no liability for the material available on those websites
or on any websites they may link to. Any comments or suggestions can be sent by email to
customerservice@enslow.com.

CONTENTS

A display at the Smithsonian Institute's National Museum of African American History and Culture in Washington, DC, shows the text of the Declaration of Independence behind a Thomas Jefferson statue and a stack of bricks bearing the names of people he enslaved.

INTRODUCTION

More than two hundred years after he left office, Thomas Jefferson remains one of the most accomplished presidents in United States history. The third leader to hold the position, Jefferson wrote a large part of the Declaration of Independence, doubled the size of the United States, and organized the Lewis and Clark expedition. Countless books have been written about his many achievements.

This was the public Jefferson. The private Jefferson was another story.

The politician carefully guarded his privacy. He often returned to his Virginia estate, Monticello. There, he escaped the chaos and conflicts that characterized the newly independent America. He also enjoyed spending time in Monticello because of its beautiful surroundings, including the home that he had designed.

His private life revealed Jefferson to be a man of contradictions. As a public figure, he championed life, liberty, and the pursuit of happiness. But he enslaved human beings on his plantations. Among them was Sally Hemings. Like so many slaves who came before and after her, Hemings would have been long forgotten—but her connection to Thomas Jefferson has made her a point of interest even today.

Just what was Hemings's connection to Jefferson? Centuries later, scholars are still asking that question. But trying to answer it simply raises more questions.

What we do know is that Jefferson fathered children with his wife, Martha. She died young, and he was heartbroken afterward. We also know that Hemings had several children. But who fathered *them*? Almost all of the debate about Hemings and Jefferson centers on that question.

Was Thomas Jefferson the father, as the Hemings family said? Or was it a Jefferson relative? History provides clues, as does science and gossip. Rumors flew about Jefferson and Hemings during their lifetimes. But in the nineteenth century, no one could prove which man fathered her children.

Today, we have genetic testing. And in 1998, the results of a DNA test provided some evidence about the Hemings-Jefferson relationship. The test, though, didn't provide all the answers. It did not say definitively which Jefferson man fathered Hemings's children. That's one of the reasons the debate goes on.

While Hemings left behind no records, diaries, or letters, Jefferson left a treasure trove of letters. They, along with his actions in life, provide insight into the man he was. What kind of man promotes freedom while owning slaves? How could Jefferson be so publicly devoted to his wife's memory while privately (as the DNA suggests) having a sexual relationship with an enslaved woman?

In many ways, Sally Hemings was a mystery as well. She traveled to France and lived there with the Jefferson family. Overseas, she was free. So, why would she return to the United States and to slavery?

Examining how fate joined together Jefferson and Hemings reveals far more than the nature of their interactions or even about them as individuals. It teaches us about race in early America and how the concept continues to affect the nation today.

PUBLIC SERVANT, PRIVATE CITIZEN

Thomas Jefferson is not only one of the nation's most famous historical figures, he's also recognized as a US Founding Father. He's arguably best known for writing part of the Declaration of Independence. The document established the thirteen colonies as a new nation, separate from Great Britain. The right to freedom stands out as an important principle in the document.

Jefferson and the other Founding Fathers may have based the new nation on the idea of liberty, but they did so during a time when scores of blacks brought over from West Africa remained in bondage in the newborn country. This is why some people have referred to slavery as America's "birth defect." As a slaveholder, Jefferson contributed to the problem, and his actions then still color his legacy today. For that reason, he's not just remembered for his staggering list of political accomplishments but for his ties to the enslaved Sally Hemings.

But long before Jefferson began his political career or controversial relationship with Hemings, he was simply a boy in Virginia.

Jefferson's Early Life

Thomas Jefferson was born on April 13, 1743, in Virginia. He was the third of Peter Jefferson and Jane Randolph Jefferson's ten children. His father was a planter, mapmaker, and surveyor—a person who examines the size and scope of land. The America of Thomas's childhood was much different from the nation we know it as today. In fact, the United States of America didn't even exist then. That would come after the American Revolution. When Thomas was a boy, Virginia was one of just thirteen American colonies.

Young Thomas enjoyed activities such as reading, hiking, and spending time in nature. His love of the outdoors continued into his adulthood. He also played the violin.

When Thomas was just fourteen, tragedy struck. His father died at age forty-nine. In the 1700s, life expectancy was much

Jefferson and His Mother

Although Thomas Jefferson is well-known for the many letters he wrote and the detailed records he kept, he didn't record much about his mother, Jane Randolph Jefferson. Upon her death, he noted in a letter to his paternal uncle William Randolph that she died "after an illness of not more than an hour."[1]

Jefferson described her illness as a stroke. She died at Monticello, and Jefferson buried her there. While many of Jefferson's letters survive, no one has found any between him and his mother. This doesn't necessarily mean they never wrote each other. If they did, perhaps the letters were destroyed.

Thomas Jefferson received a well-rounded education that included music, history, literature, and several foreign languages.

Thomas Jefferson's cherished home, Monticello, is located just outside of Charlottesville, Virginia. The design of the building was heavily influenced by neoclassical architectural principles, but it also contains 18th-century design elements, as well as Jefferson's own touches.

shorter than it is today. Many people didn't live past their twenties or thirties, and infant mortality was terribly high as well.

Two years after Peter Jefferson's death, Thomas enrolled in the College of William and Mary. There, he met Patrick Henry, who would play a key role in America's fight for independence from Great Britain. Jefferson also met attorney George Wythe—a man who would play an important role in his life. Wythe served as a mentor of sorts for the fatherless student, and Jefferson began what would end up becoming a five-year apprenticeship with him. Such a long apprenticeship was uncommon at the time, when most students studied law for only two years.

In 1767, Jefferson began practicing law. He never truly embraced the profession, even though he worked in it for seven years. Instead, he saw himself as more of a planter, like his father. But Peter Jefferson had always stressed the importance of education to his children. His father's values likely motivated Thomas to leave behind agricultural life to pursue higher education.

Jefferson's efforts paid off. In 1769, he was elected to the House of Burgesses, the legislative body that governed colonial Virginia. During this time, the young lawyer accepted a case that provides some insight into the complexity of his character. On behalf of an enslaved man, he took up a "freedom suit" in 1770. Enslaved people brought such claims against their captors to win freedom. Jefferson's case involved a man born to a white mother and black father. Back then, mixed-race people were known as "mulattoes," but today the term "biracial" is considered more appropriate to describe such individuals. In eighteenth-century Virginia, a mother's legal status determined whether her child would be slave or free. So, if an enslaved woman had children, her offspring were born slaves as well.

This rule stemmed from a 1662 legal doctrine called *partus sequitur ventrem*. The Latin phrase means "that which is brought forth follows the womb." Prior to that, the law determined that children inherited the status of their father.

Jefferson argued that because the young man in the case had a free, white mother, the man should have the same status as she did. Despite his solid argument, Jefferson lost the case. But it wouldn't be the only time he took on cases involving enslaved people or tried to stop the spread of slavery during his career.

Monticello is a National Historic Landmark because of its important history.

As he settled into his career, Jefferson also made some changes to his personal life. After his father died, he'd inherited several thousand acres of land. So, in 1768, he began building Monticello, the property he called home and where he spent most of his time. A popular tourist destination, Monticello still exists today.

On January 1, 1772, Thomas Jefferson married his third cousin Martha Wayles Skelton. The couple would have six children together, but only two girls survived into adulthood. Two weeks after Thomas wed Martha, he and his bride moved to Monticello, then under construction. Although Monticello was completed that year, Jefferson constantly made additions and changes to the estate. He wanted to create something truly original. He literally paid a price for his interest in home improvement. His finances were often stretched to their limit, with debt plaguing him for much of his life.

But not all of his debt originated from his actions. For example, shortly after his marriage to Martha, her father,

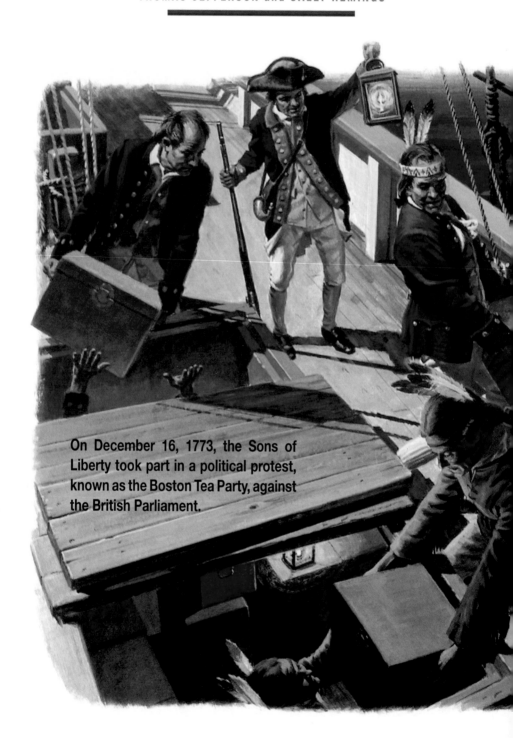

On December 16, 1773, the Sons of Liberty took part in a political protest, known as the Boston Tea Party, against the British Parliament.

John Wayles, died. This resulted in Jefferson inheriting Wayles's land. But because Wayles owed money on the land, Jefferson had to sell much of his own property to pay off this debt.

The Jeffersons also inherited Poplar Forest, which they made their second home. It was a smaller, more private property. There, Jefferson enjoyed riding horses, reading, and writing some of the many letters he penned during his life. They didn't receive many visitors there.

Although Jefferson had to settle many of his father-in-law's debts, he chose not to sell Wayles's slaves. They included Elizabeth "Betty" Hemings. Wayles fathered several of Betty Hemings's children, most notably Sally. This made Martha and Sally half-sisters, although the relationship would not have been openly acknowledged as such.

The Hemings family soon moved to Monticello.

A Political Career Begins

Jefferson stopped practicing law by the end of 1774. He didn't become a full-time gentleman farmer like he wanted due to the increasing strife between the colonists and Great Britain. Instead, he entered the world of politics.

In December 1773, growing tensions between the Massachusetts colony and the British Parliament led to the Boston Tea Party. In defiance of the Tea Act, which placed a tax on tea, protestors dumped hundreds of chests of British tea into Boston Harbor. This was one of the events that sparked the American Revolution.

Thomas Jefferson viewed all colonists as Americans, not British citizens. After the tea party, he took a leadership role in organizing resistance to British rule. He felt more comfortable writing about his views than sharing them in public. In his pamphlet "A Summary View of the Rights of British America,"

Jefferson recounted grievances against England's King George III. England viewed him as a traitor for writing the tract and took particular offense to his assertion that colonists should have the same rights as British citizens.

Many people consider Thomas Jefferson the "Father of the Declaration of Independence."

In April 1775, the Revolutionary War began between Britain and the American colonies. Jefferson spent some of the war years continuing work at Monticello. The fact that he kept so many notes about life on the estate has given historians a glimpse into Jefferson's world. He kept a detailed garden book, where he wrote down information about the weather, daily chores, and planting. Because of this, we know that the Jefferson household then consisted of one hundred and seventeen people: thirty-four were free, and eighty-three were enslaved.

Away from Monticello, America underwent some drastic changes. In June 1776, Congress named a group of five men to draft the Declaration of Independence. The men included Benjamin Franklin, John Adams, Roger Sherman, Robert Livingston—and Thomas Jefferson. The group intended to write the document in a way that allowed ordinary citizens to understand it and not just the educated and elite.

It took seventeen days to write the declaration. The men who wrote it wanted it to define "not just a country and its people, but a way of life for all humanity."[2] Jefferson authored most of the Declaration of Independence, and Congress adopted it on July 4, 1776, in Philadelphia.

Jefferson returned home to Monticello soon after. He wanted to spend more time there because his wife, Martha, was often sick. However, he continued working to promote

American independence. During that time, he drafted dozens of bills, some of which focused on general education for everyone. Otherwise, only the rich would be allowed an education, which could result in the same type of classism the colonists had criticized.

In June 1779, Jefferson became governor of Virginia. The state capital moved from Williamsburg to Richmond. In 1780, he won reelection. The following year, Jefferson had a close call. He barely escaped a group of British troops who came to Monticello to seize him.

Although Jefferson and his family eluded capture, the period afterward proved challenging. His second term as governor had ended without the Virginia Assembly electing its next governor. Jefferson viewed himself as a private citizen, but many Virginians saw him as their war governor. And because he'd run away, the public largely considered him to be a coward. He gave a speech in December 1781 to clear his name. The public criticism he endured nearly put him off politics. In fact, he might have left the spotlight altogether had his wife lived.

Grief and Politics

Martha Jefferson died on September 6, 1782, not long after giving birth to a sixth child, Lucy. Martha had grown up with two stepmothers and wanted her own children to avoid the experience. On her deathbed, she made her husband promise that he wouldn't marry again. He agreed.

Jefferson had turned down several assignments from Congress before his wife's death. Afterward, he accepted a new role as part of the American delegation, or official group, to France. Congress wanted him to take part in negotiating a peace treaty with England. If Martha had been alive, he may not have accepted the request. But the job gave him a way to keep busy and overcome his grief as a widower.

Martha Wayles Jefferson was the only child of John Wayles. She died at the age of thirty-three, before her husband became president.

The American Revolution ended in 1783. In June of that year, Jefferson went to Philadelphia, where he represented Virginia before the Confederation Congress. America's ruling body, the congress was made up of representatives chosen by state legislators. In Philadelphia, Jefferson proposed his plan to ban slavery in western territories and any future states. His proposals were defeated, but this turn of events did not hurt his political career. Instead it grew fuller. In the summer of 1784, Jefferson sailed with his daughter Martha to Paris. He had the task of negotiating commercial treaties with European countries, but he didn't feel like a skillful diplomat at first.

Then, he received bad news at the beginning of 1785. His youngest child, Lucy, had died several months before. Once again, he busied himself in his political work to cope. He adjusted to his role as diplomat, and his reputation as an outspoken defender of America grew. In reaction to Lucy's death, he sent for his daughter Polly to join him in France.

In May 1785, Jefferson was named as Benjamin Franklin's successor as the American minister to France. He enjoyed his stay in Europe very much. In 1787, Polly arrived to join him. She came with a teenaged Sally Hemings as her caretaker.

Two years later, Jefferson returned home to serve as secretary of state. In March 1790, he arrived in New York, then the US capital. As secretary of state, Jefferson had many clashes with Alexander Hamilton, who served as secretary of the treasury. The two men differed in background and personality.

Jefferson then served as vice president under President John Adams. From there, he was elected president. He served from 1801 to 1809, distinguishing himself as the first president to live in the White House. As the young nation's leader, he made his goal of expanding the United States a reality. He arranged the Lewis and Clark expedition, which gave him and other leaders a much better idea of the West's landscape, geographical makeup,

Rembrandt Peale's portrait of Thomas Jefferson shows the president looking stately and distinguished during his time in office.

Best Friends Forever

John Adams and Thomas Jefferson had been close friends for a long time. Then they both ran against each other during the 1800 presidential race. Cracks began to develop in their relationship.

Jefferson and the Democratic-Republican Party felt that Federalists like Adams were too pro-England. Adams and members of his party considered Jefferson too radical. People described the election as very ugly. Both men called each other names and repeated nasty stories about the other.

The two didn't speak for years. Eventually, though, they began writing to each other and resumed their friendship. They died within hours of each other on July 4, 1826.

and peoples. And he negotiated the Louisiana Purchase, which doubled the size of the country.

Despite his vast number of accomplishments, Jefferson happily returned to Monticello when his second presidential term ended. He left politics for good. But he wasn't finished with Monticello. He continued to pour money into restoring the property. He had to sell more land to pay off debts, but it allowed him to keep his cherished home.

Thomas Jefferson died on July 4, 1826, at age eighty-three. His death fell on the fiftieth anniversary of the document he played a pivotal role in writing—the Declaration of Independence.

KEPT WOMAN

Thomas Jefferson is one of the most studied presidents in American history. He left behind letters and a number of accomplishments that still influence public life today. But the public knows little about Sally Hemings, and much of what is known comes from the notes in Jefferson's garden book. Additionally, her children provided some information about her, as did the people enslaved with her at Monticello. She, however, did not get to tell her own story.

Sally's Early Life

Sally Hemings was born in 1773 to Betty Hemings. Before Sally was born, her mother had several children with an unknown enslaved man. However, Sally's father is widely believed to be slaveholder John Wayles.

A planter, John Wayles married three times. His first wife, Martha Eppes, brought Betty Hemings into their marriage as a gift from her parents. Martha gave birth to several children, but only one survived to adulthood. They named their daughter Martha as well. She, of course, grew up to be the future wife of President Thomas Jefferson.

After Wayles's third wife died, he didn't marry again. Historians believe he took Betty Hemings as his concubine. By definition, a concubine is a woman who's not married to a man but maintains a sexual relationship with him. She lacks the privileges of a wife and usually occupies a lower social standing than the man involved. Accordingly, such women typically do not have a say in the arrangement.

In the Virginia plantation system, families often knew when a slave owner had children with an enslaved woman. However, people didn't openly discuss the situation. To do so would have been highly improper. But men sometimes talked to other men about it in private, and women did the same within their social circles. Gossip among the slave-owning classes was normal.

Betty Hemings

Sally Hemings's mother, Betty Hemings, was the daughter of an African woman named Susannah Epps and a white English sea captain, John Hemings. According to the family's oral history, John Hemings tried to buy his newborn daughter, Betty, from her owner. But the owner refused to sell her. Then, Hemings plotted to kidnap her.

When her owner heard about this plan, he moved Betty and her mother close to the plantation house, where he could keep a close eye on them. After that, Captain Hemings gave up on the idea of taking his daughter and left the area, possibly returning to England. The captain's motives remain unclear, however. Family history says that he was less interested in raising her as his daughter and more curious about what she would look like due to her racial makeup.

Betty Hemings's mother may have escaped the concubine's fate. She was an enslaved African, but Betty's father was a British sea captain, not a slaveholder. Her father's race made Betty biracial, or a mulatto. Betty went on to have six children with John Wayles. Sally Hemings was the youngest child of this "shadow family." Sally was just a quarter black, making her what was then called a "quadroon." Although she and several siblings were more European than African, they were born into slavery because Betty was an enslaved woman.

After Wayles's death, Betty had two more children, so Sally had numerous siblings of various skin tones and ancestry. Sally was half sister to Martha Wayles because they shared the same father. But Martha was, of course, white and free.

John Wayles chose not to free any of his slaves, including his own offspring, during his lifetime or in his will. He also didn't recognize Betty Hemings's children as his own. Men who had shadow families with enslaved women commonly behaved this way. But since Wayles had so much debt when he died, it's curious that he didn't sell any of his slaves to settle it. Because many slaveholders who fathered children with slaves never acknowledged these children as their own, they sometimes sold their offspring for financial reasons or otherwise.

John Wayles died in 1773, around the time Sally was born. Her birth name was Sarah, but no record exists of her birthdate. A lack of birth records for slaves was common during this time, especially if an owner didn't keep the detailed notes that Thomas Jefferson did. If owners did record births, they typically did so in the same way they recorded buying or selling property. They viewed their enslaved workers as simply belongings.

Shortly after her father died, Martha Jefferson brought Betty Hemings and her children to Monticello. When a slave owner passed away, his slaves could be sold off as property. In many cases, slave auctions led to the fracturing of enslaved families.

Mothers and fathers, brothers and sisters, could all be sold away from each other. The Hemings family enjoyed the rare fortune of being kept together.

Sally Hemings probably arrived at Monticello as a toddler. Very little information exists about her earliest years. At age nine, in 1782, she went to the Eppes's plantation with Jefferson's youngest daughters, Polly and Lucy. Jefferson sent them there because he was preparing to go to Paris as part of his role in peace negotiations with Great Britain. Elizabeth Wayles Eppes was Martha Jefferson's half sister. But by then, Martha had died.

Lucy died in 1784, and a few years afterward, Jefferson sent for Polly to come to Paris. Since Polly was only about nine, Sally accompanied her on the long voyage from America to Europe. Just a young teen, Sally was not the first choice to care for Polly. But an older woman, Isabel Hern, had

recently had a baby and was unable to travel. So, Sally went in her place. Sally's older brother James was already in Paris with Jefferson. James was Jefferson's valet, or personal servant. He also trained as a chef to master French cuisine, and some of his recipes have survived.

In 1787, Sally and Polly arrived first in London before they traveled to Paris to meet Jefferson. John Adams's wife, Abigail, received them. According to Abigail Adams, who met

Brandon Dillard, manager of special programs at Monticello, stands in a house there where slaves lived. Members of the Hemings family likely lived in this house at some point.

the girls in London, Sally "appears good naturd."[1] Young and inexperienced, Hemings could barely meet her caretaking duties for Polly. And like all of the Hemings family, Sally didn't perform hard work on the plantation.

A 1777 painting of the Pont-Neuf in Paris depicts the bridge that crosses the Seine River. *Pont-Neuf* means "New Bridge" in English. The bridge is now a historical monument.

Returning to America

One of the biggest questions about Hemings is why she made the decision to return to America from France. After all, by leaving Paris, she was leaving freedom. When Jefferson told his family that he was preparing to return home to Monticello, how did Sally react to this news?

Like most of the enslaved people at Monticello, she was very familiar with Jefferson. She may have known that he didn't like conflict and that the best way to approach him about the issue was with terms both of them could accept for her return. For Sally, this may very well have been freedom for her future children.

Sally spent a little more than two years in France. She and her brother lived as free people there because France didn't recognize slavery. Why then did she return to America, where she knew she would live as someone's property?

Since she didn't record her reasons, historians speculate that pregnancy led to her decision. Sally was about sixteen when she returned to the United States and to a life in bondage. Soon after, she gave birth to her first child.

Many historians today believe that Hemings was Jefferson's concubine for many years and that he was likely the father of at least one of her children. Some scholars believe he fathered all of them. Although the true nature of Jefferson and Hemings's relationship can't be completely proven, we do know that even if Jefferson had wanted Hemings to be his wife, she couldn't have been. At that time, the law prohibited people of different races from marrying each other.

The Promise

No portraits exist of Sally Hemings. But people who knew her described her as "very handsome…mighty near white."[2] More European than African in racial makeup, it's not surprising that she was so light-skinned. She had "long straight hair down her back,"[3] and some people on Monticello called her "Dashing Sally."[4]

But what was she like as a person? Was she a friendly girl who liked to laugh? Or was she more serious? Slave owners didn't usually take much into account about enslaved people beyond their physical traits. How slaves performed their duties mattered more than their personalities, since they were not regarded as really human. Slaveholders did worry if slaves became sick—simply because such slaves might be unable to complete their work.

Only First Lady Abigail Adams provided any trace of what Sally was like, and even her account was brief. After Sally had her first child, she gave birth to six more children. Scholars believe that one child died in infancy and two more died in childhood. Four of her seven children lived to adulthood, and all grew up with her on the Monticello estate.

The fact that Jefferson didn't sell any of Hemings's children is telling. After all, he did sell members of other enslaved families away. While he bristled at the idea of selling young children away from their mothers, he felt that twelve-year-olds were old enough to leave their parents.

So, why did he keep the Hemings family together? He wrote many letters but never explained his reasons for this unusual decision. Some scholars say that Jefferson might have felt an attachment to the Hemings children. Also, Betty Hemings and several of her children had a long relationship with the Wayles and Jefferson families alike. They may have occupied completely different classes, but they were familiar to each other. In fact, they were family.

Jefferson never directly addressed the rumors about his ties to Hemings. As a result, he also didn't acknowledge her children as anything more than human chattel, or people he owned. Individuals close to both families maintain that Jefferson never hinted that he favored the Hemingses. Although he freed others, he never gave Sally Hemings her freedom. But he did show preference to the Hemingses in some ways. None of them performed hard labor like the other slaves on the plantation. Jefferson also insisted that none of the Hemings women do heavy farm work. If he sent any Hemings slaves to work on other farms, he didn't want them performing hard work there, either.

We may not know much about Hemings beyond the number of children she had, but her son Madison Hemings discussed her in an 1873 interview with an Ohio newspaper. By his account, Sally Hemings didn't want to leave France and return to America. She was beginning to learn French and wanted her freedom in that European country. Jefferson, however, made her an "extraordinary" promise, convincing her to head back to the United States.[5] What was this extraordinary promise? Madison said it was the promise of her future children's freedom upon adulthood.

A typical slave cabin at Monticello was a small, modest space. This sparse room contrasts with the the plantation's "big house," where the slaveholder's family lived.

After Jefferson's death, his daughter inherited Monticello, but she also inherited a lot of debt. The estate passed through several hands until the Thomas Jefferson Foundation bought it in 1923.

> *Sally Hemings had started to learn French when she left Paris.*

Some historians also believe that Hemings wanted to be close to her family. Whatever the reasons were, she came back to America and lived the rest of her life there. Sally Hemings was never officially given her freedom. Instead, Jefferson's daughter, Martha Jefferson Randolph (Hemings's niece), gave an elderly Hemings "her time." This was an unofficial, undocumented way of giving an older slave freedom. In her later years, Hemings lived with two of her adult sons in Charlottesville, Virginia. She died sometime in 1835, at about age sixty-one.

Through her several surviving children, she provided a lasting legacy that continues to be tied to the Jefferson name. Historians haven't always accepted or recognized this connection. And since neither Hemings nor Jefferson provided details about the type of relationship they had, scholars have had to speculate. Some believe in Jefferson's complete devotion to his late wife, Martha. In contrast, a growing number believe that Jefferson and Hemings had an intimate relationship after Martha's death.

THE TRIP TO PARIS

Jefferson scholars agree that his years in Europe were important politically and professionally. As part of a delegation representing the newly formed United States, Jefferson joined an influential group of other Americans who helped form relationships and alliances. The group wasn't always warmly received, as King George III gave John Adams a rather chilly reception in London. For the most part, Jefferson enjoyed his time in France. It took him some time to get used to the different customs. But over time, he grew much more comfortable in his role.

The Journey to Paris

Thomas Jefferson went to Paris in July 1784 as part of the US delegation to negotiate treaties, or agreements. This group included John Adams and Benjamin Franklin. Jefferson's wife, Martha, had died just two years before. Many people, including some of his friends, believed that he took the assignment as a way to overcome his grief. He also had more time to devote to his political career after his wife's death. Previously, he may

John Trumbull's portrait of Jefferson, circa 1788, depicts Jefferson wearing the typical attire in France during that time. Jefferson supported the French Revolution but not its more violent protests.

have felt guilty leaving the country for an extended time because it would have meant leaving behind an ailing wife.

Jefferson left Monticello in the hands of his entrusted slaves, and he departed for Europe with his daughter Martha, also called Patsy. His other daughters, Polly and Lucy, stayed at Eppington Plantation under the care of their aunt and cousins.

Jefferson grew to enjoy his time in France. No one knows how long he might have stayed there without sending for Polly if his youngest daughter, Lucy, hadn't died from whooping cough in October 1784. Making matters worse, months passed before Jefferson learned of Lucy's passing. The letters that his sister-in-law and brother-in-law, Elizabeth and Francis Eppes, sent him about Lucy's tragic fate didn't actually arrive until May 1785. During that era, it could take weeks, sometimes months, for mail to get from one country to another. Even so, it's still incredible that letters bearing such horrible news took six months to be delivered. The lag time meant that Jefferson didn't grieve his daughter until months after her death. He felt angry that he didn't learn about her demise sooner.

The terrible fate of his youngest daughter gave Jefferson the idea to send for nine-year-old Polly. He didn't set his plan into motion right away because he thought that he would soon return to America. Not long after getting word about Lucy's death, however, Jefferson received more news: he would replace Benjamin Franklin as the next American minister to France.

Polly, by all accounts, greatly enjoyed her time with her aunt and cousins on Eppington Plantation, so she hardly jumped at the chance to travel to France to be with her father. It took some convincing on Jefferson's part to get Polly onto the ship. It also took some time. Polly and caretaker Sally Hemings didn't board a boat for Europe until May 1787.

Sally was not the first choice to supervise the lively Polly. For one thing, she was little more than a child herself. She was only

The house at Eppington Plantation is the resting place of Lucy Elizabeth Jefferson, Thomas Jefferson's daughter who died in toddlerhood. Eppington is in Chesterfield County, Virginia.

about fourteen years old. Yet, when an older enslaved woman could not make the trip, Sally took her place.

Convincing Polly to get on a Europe-bound ship required a bit of deception. Her relatives led her to believe that her cousins would travel with her. They had to tell her this story because the young girl became "almost hysterical" when anyone brought up the idea of her leaving.[1] Once Polly fell asleep on the ship, her cousins slipped away and returned home. When she awakened, her family had vanished. Only Sally remained by her side. Who knows what thoughts ran through little Polly's mind as a result of this disappearing act.

The five long weeks spent onboard may have been very difficult for both girls. As it turns out, Polly grew very attached to the ship's captain, Andrew Ramsay. Polly and Sally were the only girls on the voyage, so they probably received special treatment. And just as Polly had grown extremely attached to her aunt and cousins, she grew very fond of Captain Ramsay. Once the voyage ended, Polly's receiving party, which included Abigail Adams, had to use all types of tricks to persuade her to leave her new friend.

Once Polly was in the care of Abigail Adams, a question arose: what should be done about Sally Hemings? Adams felt Sally could return to the United States, and Captain Ramsay agreed, but the two likely had different reasons. Adams may have thought that the pretty teen would be too much of a distraction if she stayed in Europe. But a distraction for whom—Thomas Jefferson? On the other hand, if Sally returned to the United States alone, she may have been the only girl present. While traveling to France, her role as Polly's caretaker had offered her some security, but if she journeyed back alone, that protection would be absent. Her status and her race could have put her in jeopardy.

Adams left the decision about Sally's fate to Jefferson. He decided that she should stay in France with her brother, James. Because Sally Hemings didn't leave detailed notes about her experience—it's unclear if she could read and write—we have no idea what she thought when she landed in Europe. We do know that life abroad presented her with a much different way of life.

Life Overseas

How James and Sally Hemings must have cherished the chance to visit France! In the United States, they were Jefferson's "property," but France did not recognize slavery. Overseas, the siblings received a small wage while working for the politician. James Hemings worked as a servant and chef-in-training,

Paris's Champs-Élysées remains one of the most famous locales in the city and is well known around the world.

and Sally worked as a maid and companion for Jefferson's two daughters.

The Hemingses could have petitioned for their freedom in France and lived there as free people. France didn't officially ban slavery until 1794, but the European nation had ended slavery "in principle" during its revolution. Slaves could go to court and ask for their freedom, and in many cases, the courts approved these requests. So why didn't James and Sally stay in France, where they would be recognized as free people of color? Why would they choose to return to America and a life of slavery? Their exact reasons may never be known. Sally's eventual pregnancy surely played a role as well as the supposed promises that Jefferson made to both Sally and her brother.

The fact that Sally became pregnant during her stay abroad raises questions about her living quarters there. Where did the teenager live for the two years she spent in France? We don't

Sally's Activities in France

What did Sally Hemings do during her time in Paris? While her duties mostly included working as a maidservant and attendant to Jefferson's two daughters, she surely had time to herself while the girls were away at their boarding school.

During her free time, Sally pursued activities such as learning French. She also learned needlework and clothing care. These were important skills since she worked mostly as the Jefferson girls' maid. Jefferson paid her about 12 livres, or $2, per month. This was about half the amount her brother James earned as Jefferson's cook.

exactly know. She could have lived with her brother at the Jefferson residence at the Hôtel de Langeac, and she very likely spent some of her time with Jefferson's daughters at their convent school.

As an older woman, Hemings often talked about her years in France.

We do know that Jefferson spent some money on material for her clothing. While he didn't spend nearly the amount for Sally's attire as he did on his daughters' apparel, he purchased enough to make her look like a credible caretaker. Jefferson probably wanted Sally to accompany one or both girls to events that required her to present herself as a well-dressed companion to well-bred young ladies.

During the more than two years Sally Hemings spent in France, she began to learn the language. Her brother James hired a tutor to learn French. Meanwhile, Jefferson also paid for Sally's smallpox inoculation (similar to a vaccination) to prevent her from getting the disease. The amount of 240 francs for this was considered a large sum of money. He might have done this out of simple charity and kindness, or he may have done it because he wanted her to stay well enough to work. In any case, the money he spent raises questions for people who argue about the true nature of their relationship. Would he have spent so much money on her clothing and inoculation if he viewed her as mere property? He may have, given that losing his property to disease would have also cost him money.

If Jefferson indeed began a sexual relationship in France with Sally, how did it begin? Historians know little about the interactions between the two there, but if they turned sexual in nature, Sally had no decision in the matter. Her young age and the fact that Jefferson had enslaved her and her family meant that she had no choice over the course of her life, let alone over her own body. While Jefferson may have felt entitled to Sally's body, social norms meant that he would not have been able to openly have a sexual relationship with the teenager in France. He was much older than her, still very much a white man, and a US diplomat. If news got out about Jefferson and his teenaged slave, it would have led to an unwelcome scandal. More than two centuries later, though, it is common knowledge that Sally was pregnant by the time she returned to America.

Before DNA evidence proved otherwise, many of Jefferson's defenders refused to link any Jefferson male—including Thomas—to Sally Hemings's children. Once genetic testing confirmed a link to "a male" in the Jefferson line to at least one of Sally's offspring, then his defenders tried to place the blame on his nephews or other relatives.

The thirty-year age difference that separated Jefferson and Sally does not mean no sexual relationship occurred between the two of them. Unfortunately, slaveholders commonly had sexual relations with the girls and women they enslaved. Now, we refer to such an abuse of power as rape. According to the age of consent laws in

This is an engraving of the courtyard at the Madelonnettes Convent in Paris, similar to the convent school, Pentemont Abbey, that Martha and Polly attended in France.

Sally's Smallpox Inoculation

Soon after Sally Hemings arrived in France, Thomas Jefferson paid a physician, Dr. Sutton, to give her a smallpox inoculation. This wasn't as simple or quick as giving someone a shot. During that time, an inoculation lasted some weeks, and the person receiving the inoculation lived separately from other people.

Although inoculation was expensive, Jefferson probably felt it was necessary to prevent Sally from getting the deadly disease. Many people who caught smallpox died. Those who lived sometimes ended up blind.

Sally had only been in France a short time when Jefferson sent her away for this medical procedure. She probably found the ordeal difficult since she had to go through it alone.

many US states today, a young teen is not old enough to consent to a sexual relationship with an adult.

Then a recent widower, Jefferson may have reasoned that he needed sexual companionship and forced Sally into the role of mistress. He probably wouldn't have had a free, white mistress, even in France. But like Abigail Adams, he felt some shock after arriving in France and learning that people there were much less reserved about such matters than they were in America. He wrote to family friend Eliza House Trist, "The domestic bonds here are absolutely done away."[2]

Historians argue over the type of bond Jefferson had with the domestic servant to whom history has forever linked him. The "relationship" could have been little more than a convenient arrangement in which Sally played the role—willingly or not—of concubine. Or it may have been more. Her surviving children

Abigail Smith Adams, wife of President John Adams, was one of the few people who gave a public account of Sally Hemings's personality and demeanor.

seem to suggest that the relationship was more than a simple act of convenience, no matter how it started.

It's unclear what Sally's life was like in France. We don't know if she made any friends there or if her role as companion and maid kept her too busy to form any bonds outside of the ones she already had. She may have felt lonely in a foreign country, although her brother's presence may have provided some comfort. His enslavement meant that James Hemings was just as powerless as Sally was. He could not stop Jefferson from pursuing his sister sexually. And because it's unclear where Sally lived abroad, we don't know how much James knew about her interactions with Jefferson. Sally and the politician may have only interacted in public occasionally, making her eventual pregnancy a surprise to all around her.

In 1789, a pregnant Sally and her brother left France and returned to the United States.

THE CONTROVERSY THEN

When we look closely at Jefferson's writings and his actions, his views on slavery seem to contradict his views on freedom. He wrote much of the Declaration of Independence, which stated very clearly the colonists' desire for "liberty," even the "pursuit of happiness." These aren't just desires; Jefferson considered them to be rights. Perhaps most important of all is the statement that "all men are created equal."

The definition of slavery is the opposite of all of these concepts. So how can the man who was such a champion of freedom and liberty be the same one who enslaved people and used slave labor to build his cherished home?

Jefferson on Slaves and Slavery

Jefferson owned slaves, but he also argued in court for freedom for slaves. In 1770, he took up his first freedom suit on behalf of a young mulatto man, and it wasn't the last time he took on such a case. Jefferson had tried unsuccessfully to put into law a ban on the spread of slavery in new states. So, why didn't he free his own slaves? How could he want freedom for all men but still own them? He likely considered slavery to be morally wrong but not so much that he refused to profit from slave labor.

Like many other white people of his time, Jefferson didn't consider black men and women to be equal to white men and women. The differences for him went deeper than skin. He believed that black people simply weren't as intelligent as white people. His white supremacist beliefs and the financial gains slavery afforded him likely led Jefferson to continue keeping blacks in bondage on Monticello while taking measures to curb slavery in other contexts.

Taken collectively, Jefferson's views, actions, and writings make it difficult for scholars to form conclusions about his relationship to slavery. Some people have described him as a kindly master. But can anyone who would deprive another human being of liberty really be kind? Jefferson may have

Poplar Forest

Jefferson returned to Monticello (the Italian word for "little mount") as much as possible, but he also spent time at his second home, Poplar Forest. He inherited it after his father-in-law's death, as the property had belonged to John Wayles and then passed along to Martha Wayles Jefferson.

Thomas Jefferson used this second plantation to earn some income, and he grew tobacco and wheat there. Slaves who worked on the property also raised livestock, or animals, for profit. The shape of the main house is octagonal, or eight-sided, which was very unusual when first built. One of his grandsons took over the property a few years before Jefferson's death.

Poplar Forest became a National Historic Landmark in 1971.

been unwilling to truly consider the state of enslaved Americans because he had quietly profited from their work for years.

Although Jefferson spent nearly his entire life interacting with enslaved people—his own "property" as well as the slaves of other families—some of his writings suggest that black people and white people should live

> *To Jefferson, the separation of whites and blacks seemed best for both races.*

separately. He "recommended resettling blacks outside of the continental United States."[1] In 1801, he wrote to James Monroe that a location such as the West Indies would be a good fit for black people. If the West Indies didn't work out, Africa could, as a last resort.

It's easy to see why Jefferson accepted slavery, including enjoying the profits from it, when we consider his views on race. Look at some of the content in his book *Notes on the State of Virginia*, which he first published in France in 1785. He wrote it partly to contradict the idea that America was inferior to Europe. Jefferson constantly defended anything American, and he made several points detailing accomplishments of men such as George Washington and Benjamin Franklin.

In this book, he didn't present slavery in a good light. He said that slavery had destroyed "the morals" of white people in Virginia and that the institution had "destroyed the industriousness of whites."[2] Jefferson suggested that white men would grow lazy if their slaves performed all hard labor for them. He also seemed to make a case for why some enslaved people resorted to "thievery." He claimed that they stole because they had little choice in the matter; it wasn't due to a lack of morals. Keep in mind that slaves could be labeled

CONTENTS.

Jefferson's *Notes on the State of Virginia* promoted what he felt were America's best traits. It also included his disparaging views about how blacks and whites are seemingly different.

thieves just for running away. Their own bodies were deemed "stolen property" in this context.

While Jefferson clearly argued that slavery was damaging, he also made several negative statements about enslaved people or blacks generally. He viewed people of African descent as *different*. He wrote that white people were more attractive than black people due to their "flowing hair" and "more elegant" bodies.[3] Jefferson suggested that black people didn't tire as easily from work. He said their lack of fatigue made them more likely to stay up late at night

> Jefferson said that slavery had destroyed "the morals" of white people in Virginia.

taking part in silly amusements despite having to rise early in the morning for work. Given that black people provided slave labor for whites from sunup to sundown, however, the nights offered the only opportunity for them to spend time together.

So, how did Jefferson think black men and women related to one another? He argued that blacks showed love and affection differently from how whites did. He claimed that white people expressed themselves in more tender and sentimental ways, while strong emotions drove the actions of black people. In short, blacks relied too much on their feelings instead of their intellect. He also reported that black people possessed little imagination and that their reasoning abilities fell far below those of whites. To him, this was all due to nature. And black people couldn't change their natures. Today, some people still share Jefferson's views, but they'd be called white supremacists for sharing them openly. Sadly, black people continue to have to prove that they're just as human as whites or anyone else.

Jefferson evidently understood that his views against blacks were biased. In other parts of *Notes on the State of Virginia*, he makes a point to say that his opinions were only that—and that studies needed to be carried out to prove that white people were superior to black people. He suggested that enslaved people might, in fact, pretend to be less intelligent than they really were. Whites feared educated black people and forbade them to read and write, so enslaved blacks may have very well pretended to be unintelligent to appease their masters. In addition to pointing out that blacks sometimes feigned ignorance, Jefferson acknowledged that blacks and whites showed no difference in memory. The groups were equals in their ability to remember things, he said.

Note that Jefferson's views have no scientific basis and that even branches of science, such as eugenics, have been used to make unfounded generalizations about people of color, the poor, mentally ill, and others. Today, researchers say that race is just a social construct, meaning that no fundamental differences exist between so-called racial groups.

Using slave labor for farming was considered the most profitable way for landowners to expand from small farms to large plantations.

In his book, Jefferson expressed many views about slavery, enslaved people, and blacks (some blacks were free). In his farm book, which was not for public consumption, he usually only described enslaved people in terms of characteristics such as "trustworthiness or unreliability, intelligence or stupidity, sobriety or drunkenness." He made these notes simply to grade the people he enslaved on their work performance.[4] He did not leave such notes very often, and when he did, he referred to the people he held in bondage solely by their first names and often with nicknames. This illustrates that he did not really consider them as individuals. He cared mostly about whether their work performance would be a help or a hindrance to him.

Did Jefferson consider Sally Hemings to be a black woman? Keep in mind that she looked more white than black—because she was. Her mother was biracial, and John Wayles, reported to be her father, was white. That meant that Hemings was three-quarters white and one-quarter black. This very likely made her more appealing to Jefferson than a purely black slave would have been, given his Eurocentric views of beauty. His views on race may also explain why he seemed to favor the entire Hemings clan. He spared them from hard labor at Monticello and anywhere else they went. Presumably, almost all of the Hemings slaves were light-skinned. Even the children that Betty Hemings reportedly had with an enslaved man were probably lighter in complexion than slaves who worked in the fields.

Jefferson might have found it easier to accept his attraction to Sally Hemings because she was so light-skinned. Based on his writings, it's unlikely that he would have had the same type of relationship with an enslaved woman who looked less European than Hemings did. It's very probable that Hemings's physical appearance played a big part in Jefferson making her his concubine. In fact, many mixed-race enslaved women found themselves in similar situations with slaveholders.

James Callender Investigates

The public didn't learn about Jefferson's supposed relationship with Sally Hemings until a scandalous story broke in 1802. By that time, however, the relationship was well known to people close to the Jefferson family and familiar with Monticello. Like other prominent men in plantation culture, particularly slaveholders, Jefferson could be "forgiven" this relationship as long as he kept it quiet and didn't openly flaunt it. Even though a 1662 Virginia law threatened "stiff fines" against "any Christian who" carried on a relationship with a "Negro man or woman," it's unclear how many people were actually fined under this statute.[5] Masters who had children with their slaves, in particular, would have suffered if this law had truly

The Rumor Mill

Well before James Callender published his sensational story in 1802, rumors about Jefferson and Hemings existed. No one knows if anyone asked Jefferson directly if he fathered Hemings's children. If they did, this conversation is lost to history.

After Callender's story came out, people continued to talk about Jefferson and Hemings, and they're still talking about it today. It's become a mix of fact and fiction. In some cases, even facts don't change people's minds. However, since neither Jefferson nor Hemings openly spoke about their connection, their descendants, historians, and other interested parties have shaped their story. While DNA evidence links "a male Jefferson" to Hemings, other information about the pair's relationship has been used to add more pieces to this complex puzzle.

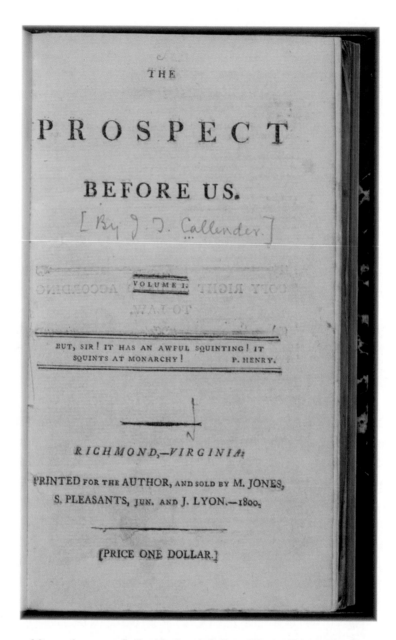

After James Callender's relationship with Jefferson soured, the journalist moved into attack mode against the president, publicizing his relationship with Sally Hemings.

been enacted. In most cases, white men who had relationships and children with black women (enslaved or free) weren't fined. Although white men who engaged in miscegenation risked legal punishment, the risk of public exposure and loss of one's reputation was more frightening than any fine.

For years, the rumors about Jefferson and Hemings just remained part of plantation life gossip. Then, in 1802, a journalist named James T. Callender linked Jefferson and Hemings in public and on paper.

Callender left his native Scotland in 1793 for fear of being jailed for treason. He'd published a pamphlet that pushed for his country's independence from Britain (much like the colonists). He continued his journalism work in America. At first, he was on good terms with Jefferson, although the two men weren't exactly friends. Jefferson, like other political leaders, had doubts about how Callender worked. The journalist's style invited confrontation.

However, Callender supported Jefferson's candidacy for president. The men exchanged several letters, and Callender expressed feelings of alliance with Jefferson. This changed in 1800 after Callender was sentenced to nine months in jail. He'd been charged under the Sedition Act. Writing negatively about the government was one offense that could land a person in jail under this act. Callender had written several nasty pieces about various political leaders, especially John Adams. Along with the jail term, Callender had to pay a $200 fine, enough to nearly bankrupt him. After Jefferson defeated Adams in the presidential election of 1800, Callender believed that the new president would pay his fees. By criticizing Adams, he thought he'd helped Jefferson win the election. Callender also wanted Jefferson to appoint him to the position of postmaster.

As president, Jefferson pardoned journalists who had been jailed due to the Sedition Act. He also saw to it that Callender received his fine money back. But by then, the relationship between the two men had soured. Firstly, Jefferson never answered any of Callender's letters while the journalist sat in jail. Callender had written to Jefferson often. He'd also become ill in prison. Secondly, it took many months before Callender received his money. By then, he'd lost patience with Jefferson. He thought he'd helped the Republican Party. He'd done the work that the politicians wanted to avoid. They didn't want to get their hands dirty by resorting to mud-slinging, but they had happily allowed Callender to do it. In the end, he felt abandoned and angry.

In September 1802, Callender published a story in the *Richmond Recorder* accusing Jefferson of having an intimate relationship with Hemings. Under the heading "The President Again," Callender not only said that Jefferson had been keeping a concubine for several years, the journalist even named her. He said that the two had several children together.

Since Jefferson was just in his first term as president at the time, Callender undoubtedly hoped that this story, and the scandal, would ruin the politician. This didn't turn out to be the case. The public largely dismissed it as just another rumor, likely because Jefferson never directly responded to the story or other rumors about his relationship with Hemings. Despite the scandalous claims Callender made, Jefferson's reputation stayed intact.

So how did Jefferson survive Callender's allegations? Why didn't the journalist's article ruin Jefferson's political career? Some people simply didn't believe the story. They didn't think a man in Jefferson's position was capable of such behavior. They idolized the president and viewed Callender's report as nothing more than petty gossip.

People familiar with how interracial relationships unfolded in the antebellum South viewed Jefferson's relationship with

Political cartoons are nothing new, as this satirical image shows. In it, Jefferson is portrayed as a rooster and Hemings is the hen.

Hemings as just another "open secret." In other words, they acknowledged such relationships in private but not in public. Also, other men in Jefferson's family, including his late father-in-law, had relationships with enslaved women. Some people thought Jefferson was simply behaving the way other men in his circle had.

Finally, some people didn't believe Callender's story because he had such a bad reputation. Many considered him a yellow journalist, or someone who printed more gossip and lies than truth. And how did Callender happen to come by this information about Jefferson? The journalist's dislike of black people and miscegenation was well known. He wouldn't have approached any of the enslaved people at Monticello about the rumors. Instead, he probably picked up the gossip from white men at social gatherings in taverns or markets. These men may have taken part in the very race-mixing that Callender hated.

Because miscegenation was so prevalent in society, making a public matter of Jefferson's open secret was not enough to derail the politician's reputation and career.

ALL OF HEMINGS'S CHILDREN

Sally Hemings had seven children, and four survived into adulthood. Three sons and one daughter eventually left Monticello and formed lives of their own as free people.

Four Survivors

Sally gave birth to her first child sometime in 1790. No name for the child is on record. Many scholars believe the infant died soon after birth, but not everyone agrees. Sally then had a girl named Harriet Hemings who lived from 1795 to 1797.

Next, Hemings had William Beverley Hemings, born in 1798. Another daughter lived only from 1799 to 1800. After that, Hemings had a second Harriet, born in 1801; James Madison, born in 1805; and finally Thomas Eston, born in 1808. The boys were better known by their middle names.

Beverley, Harriet, Madison, and Eston grew up, although the full details of their lives, including when they died, are spotty. But Hemings's first child has proven the most mysterious. What became of the baby? Did her firstborn really die?

When Callender's story broke in 1802, he claimed that Jefferson and Hemings had a son together named Tom. Callender even called the boy "President Tom" in his series of attacks on Jefferson. The journalist said that Tom was twelve years old, which fits the timeline if Hemings's firstborn actually survived.

While there's no recorded evidence of a Tom surviving into adulthood, the family of Thomas C. Woodson relied on oral history to support these claims. They claim that Woodson was Jefferson's son and that he left Monticello as a young boy. He eventually made his way to Ohio, where he became a farmer.

But is he really Thomas Jefferson's son?

No records exist of a Hemings child named Tom. Jefferson reportedly didn't keep a farm book from 1783 to 1794, so there's no reason to think he intentionally kept the child a secret by not recording his birth. In addition, the descendants of Madison Hemings maintain that his mother's first child didn't live. This makes it very likely that the infant didn't survive. Moreover, the 1998 DNA study does not link Woodson to the Jefferson family.

That one of Hemings's children was named James Madison and another was named Thomas Eston is interesting. Do these names give more weight to the idea that Jefferson fathered them? In 1873, Madison gave an interview to an Ohio newspaper explaining how he got his name. In it, he said Mrs. James Madison named him at birth.

"Mrs. Madison happened to be at Monticello at the time of my birth, and begged the privilege of naming me, promising my mother a fine present for the honor. She consented, and Mrs. Madison dubbed me by the name I now acknowledge, but like many promises of white folks to the slaves she never gave my mother anything."

During the same interview, Madison named Thomas Jefferson as his father. He provided some details about what

Dolley Madison was the wife of President James Madison. She was well known for her graceful manner as well as boosting her husband's popularity.

According to Madison Hemings (Sally's son), Dolley Madison asked to name him when he was born.

it was like growing up on Monticello with Jefferson, who didn't or couldn't acknowledge him as a son. Madison also described growing up alongside his white relatives.[1] He said that Jefferson was an even-tempered man who rarely got angry but at times became irritated. He said that his father rarely got sick, and that he knew him mostly in the domestic sphere and not as a famous politician. Due to the agreement his parents made before he and his siblings were born, Madison said that the Hemings children were spared from leading the lives of slaves.

Madison's brother, Thomas Eston, also had a name that stands out. His family called him simply Eston. When enslaved people had children, they often gave them names similar to the families that owned them, but Hemings didn't name him Thomas after Jefferson. Instead, the name Thomas was just a family name that she used.

Nearly all the Hemings children had names closely connected to the Jefferson and Randolph lines (Jefferson's mother's maiden name was Randolph). Why didn't the children have the name Jefferson? It was common practice to give enslaved people the surnames (or last names) of their masters. However, the Hemings family kept their name, even when John Wayles had owned them.

When Jefferson recorded the births of Hemings's children, he didn't note the father's name, which he often did for other slave births. Instead, he left this space blank for all of her offspring.

Martha's Dilemma

Jefferson may not have been openly affectionate with Hemings's children, but no one doubted that the enslaved family received special treatment. Just as he'd done with Sally Hemings's siblings and half siblings, Jefferson made sure her children did not perform hard labor. But Jefferson could not have paid extra attention to Hemings's children, especially once his married daughter Martha (now Martha Jefferson Randolph) and her family moved back to Monticello. To do so would have been considered inappropriate at that time and in that environment. It might have angered Martha as well.

A Broken Promise

Madison Hemings told an Ohio newspaper the story of Dolley Madison giving him his name. He doesn't tell the story to show pride in sharing the name with a former president but to point out that Madison supposedly promised Sally Hemings a gift if she named her baby after Madison's husband. After giving birth, however, Hemings never received a gift.

Madison Hemings felt that Dolley Madison had treated his mother badly by breaking this promise. The only way he would have known about this conversation is through his mother. Perhaps Hemings told her son this story to show him that some people are unreliable and think nothing of breaking their word to another.

Dolley Madison might have gone back on her word to Hemings because the two women didn't occupy the same social class. She may have figured that she didn't have to keep a promise to an enslaved woman.

Martha might have denied that Hemings's children were her half siblings, but she probably noticed they looked like her. Several other people remarked on the resemblance, including family members, slaves at Monticello, and visitors to the plantation. Perhaps Martha thought that her father's nephews or another Jefferson male had a relationship with Hemings, or she told herself that enough times to make it sound believable.

In her world, a lot of race-mixing had taken place. Although proper ladies wouldn't openly discuss miscegenation, they couldn't ignore the obvious. The "open secret" of miscegenation produced very visible results while remaining invisible in the sense that no one commented on it openly. Perhaps white society felt that if they didn't talk about race-mixing, it didn't really exist. But there was another reason that whites did not discuss their enslaved relatives: money. Children born into a marriage, otherwise known as legal heirs, wouldn't want to share their inheritance with children born outside of it. Illegitimate children, or those born to an unmarried

Jefferson's slaves maintained vegetable gardens at Monticello, where they tended crops for him. They also grew a variety of flowers on the grounds.

couple, usually had no legal rights to money or property. This included illegitimate white children as well as mixed-race or black children.

Occasionally, a slaveholder might provide an education for his mulatto children; sometimes, he sent these offspring to Europe. In other cases, he might provide ways for them to learn a trade. These outcomes happened rarely. In the majority of cases where a white man had children with an enslaved woman, he treated these offspring much like he did other slaves. This included selling them away from their mother.

Martha was extremely close to her father and idolized him. She didn't want any damaging gossip about him and Hemings to continue and made a deathbed claim that Jefferson couldn't possibly have fathered at least one of Hemings's children because he hadn't been at Monticello for fifteen months before that child's birth. This claim was later proven to be false.

Martha's Gift

People often speculate about how Martha Wayles Skelton Jefferson felt about Sally Hemings, her half sister. The two grew up together in very different circumstances. Martha Jefferson couldn't recognize Hemings as her sibling, but it seems she gave her at least one gift.

On Martha's deathbed, she presented Hemings with a small bell. This is according to Hemings family tradition, though no other details about the bell or any words exchanged between the two during this time are on record. Martha Jefferson, much like her daughter, lived beside her enslaved relatives without being able to publicly acknowledge them.

Martha Jefferson Randolph, called Patsy, was the only child of Thomas and Martha Jefferson who survived past the age of twenty-five. She had her father's red hair.

Martha may have disapproved of her father's relationship with Hemings, but she chose to give the enslaved woman "her time." This allowed Hemings to live nearly the final decade of her life in an unofficial freedom.

The Free World

In 1822, brother and sister Beverley and Harriet Hemings "ran away" from Monticello. Jefferson didn't go after them or send anyone to bring them back. They weren't actual runaway slaves, which explains why Jefferson never pursued them, although he did note their disappearance in his farm book.

If it's true that Jefferson made promises to Hemings to free her children upon adulthood, this was a way he could do so privately. Jefferson didn't want to spark any speculation about their parentage, especially after the publication of Callender's controversial stories. Although many people refused to believe Callender's articles, whispers of Jefferson's relationship with Hemings continued.

Beverley left first, with Harriet following some months later. Jefferson gave his overseer some money to give to Harriet to help her on her travels. This definitely didn't appear to be a runaway situation, but it provided Jefferson with a quiet way to keep his promise to Hemings without raising alarms. Allowing Beverley and Harriet to escape, however, didn't help Jefferson's financial situation. As human chattel, or property, their disappearances were recorded as losses.

Historians know only that both Beverley and Harriet married white people and then lived the rest of their lives as whites. They disappeared into white society, with no known records of when or how they died.

Thomas Eston Hemings was Sally Hemings's last child. His descendants provided the DNA samples that established a direct link between him and a male Jefferson descendant. It's not possible to make comparisons directly between Thomas Jefferson and any of Hemings's children, of course, and testing the Y-chromosomes (unique to males) was the closest these tests could come.

Although Jefferson adored his oldest grandson, a boy who shared his name (Thomas Jefferson Randolph), he shared few physical or character traits with this legal heir. It was Jefferson's youngest child with Hemings who more closely fit the "like father, like son" saying.

Eston Hemings was described as being "a near copy of Jefferson facially and physically in terms of his height and build."[2] He loved music, as did Jefferson. When freed in Jefferson's will, Eston left Monticello and he took the name E. H. Jefferson.

Jefferson didn't free Sally Hemings, but in his will, he did free Madison and Eston, along with a few other enslaved men who were members of the Hemings family. More than one hundred other slaves were sold to settle his debts. He also made provisions that allowed these free men to continue living in the state.

An 1806 amendment to Virginia's manumission law stated that if a master freed a slave, the newly freed person had to leave Virginia within one year. If the person continued to live in the state, he or she ran the risk of being re-enslaved. Naturally, this made it difficult for owners to free their slaves because most people who gained freedom didn't want to leave their families and connections behind. This greatly brought down the rates of manumission, or setting enslaved people free. While freedom was a great desire for many slaves, it would have been extremely painful to leave their families and have to start life over in a new place. They would have to leave wives, husbands, and children. The men who drafted these laws were well aware of this and counted on a person not wanting to separate from his family. The number of freed slaves fell in a big way due to this law.

Knowing about the law, Jefferson's will included a petition to allow the men to stay in Virginia, where they would be near their families.

"Passing" is when people of one race pass themselves off as another race. Passing almost always involved black people who had complexions and hair textures that made others believe they were white. The majority of blacks who passed did so to improve their lot in life. As white people, they could avoid the fierce discrimination that kept blacks in the lower rungs of society. Instead of suffering all the mistreatment and violence that blacks commonly endured, people who passed for white could life lives of privilege, or at least lives free of blatant racism. They married into white society and had children who looked white. They often cut off all contact with their black relatives. It was a painful choice but a necessary one if they wanted to conceal their real racial identity. People who passed for white lived in constant fear that someone would uncover their secret.

It's interesting that all of Sally Hemings's children, except one, chose to pass into white society. Madison was the only one to continue to live as a person of color, although his appearance was more European than African. His siblings' decision to pass disappointed him. It's also surprising that Eston was able to pass himself off as a white man considering the description of him as "light bronze colored" with a "visible admixture" of black features.[3]

Eston Hemings was apparently "white enough to pass for white."

At that time, according to Virginia law, Eston was considered a white man, despite some obvious evidence of his African ancestry.

78

By law, he was more European than African. Although his complexion evidently wasn't light enough to give him a white appearance, he looked "white enough to pass for white."[4] His wife, too, was mixed race but looked white. Their children, therefore, looked white. As the generations went on, many of Hemings's descendants either passed completely into white society or married other mixed-race individuals.

Even some of Madison's descendants married white people, so they then disappeared into white society as well. Today, while many of Hemings's descendants look white or nearly white, others clearly display their African American heritage.

SALLY'S SACRIFICE

Reportedly beautiful, the teenaged Sally Hemings probably attracted attention when she arrived in Europe with Polly Jefferson. Because we know so little about where Sally lived in Paris and how she spent her free time, it's unclear if she bonded with the locals there. She certainly spent time with her brother James. But did she encounter free people of color, people who lived the life of her dreams?

A Chance for Freedom

Paris housed a small community of people of color. This community may have spotted Sally and James Hemings and reached out to them. Had Sally Hemings remained in France, she could have married into this community. Many of the free black people in the area lived in a small number of neighborhoods, and they were mostly young men. She would probably have had her choice of a future husband among these Frenchmen, who typically worked as servants for white families or as tradesmen.

James Hemings used some of his earnings to hire a tutor so that he could learn French. His sister began to learn the language as well. Both Hemingses may have been able to communicate with any Frenchmen of color they encountered.

Knowing what we do about slavery, it's hard to imagine why both Hemingses would return to America and continued enslavement instead of staying behind in France. Although Jefferson was technically their master and owner, he knew (and it's very probable that they learned) that they could petition for their freedom in France. In the majority of cases where enslaved people traveled to France with their owners and petitioned for their freedom, they succeeded.

Did James and Sally ever consider requesting their freedom? Did they approach Jefferson with these requests? We don't know, just as we don't know if they formed bonds with fellow people of color in Paris. What we do know is that when Jefferson returned to America, the two Hemingses returned with him.

But why?

As an enslaved teenager, Sally had virtually no power. The most power she held was probably during her years in France, where she was "free." As Jefferson prepared to return to the United States, Sally had to consider several things before making a decision about her destiny. Would she remain in France, never to see her family in Virginia again, or would she return to a life as human chattel in the United States?

If Jefferson told her that he would free her children, she must have believed him. He could have broken his promise later, as some people do. But it seems that Hemings

> *To Hemings, Jefferson "promised her extraordinary privileges" including "a solemn pledge" to free her children.*

The French Revolution took place in the 1700s. Citizens demanded equal rights across class lines.

The Mystery of Sally Hemings

Many paintings, portraits, and even sculptures of Thomas Jefferson exist. This stands in stark contrast to Sally Hemings. Not even one portrait of her exists. The very few "pictures" there are only suggest what she might have looked like, based on the handful of physical descriptions on record about her.

In addition to capturing Jefferson's image, many writers have covered the politician's life and accomplishments in hundreds of books. They've debated about the type of man he was, held endless discussions about his character, examined his family life, and much more.

On the other hand, the amount of literature on Hemings is tiny. Yet, almost anytime people talk about Jefferson, her name comes up. Although very few books chronicle her life story and no actual portraits capture her image, Hemings is far more than a minor historical figure.

knew him well enough to believe he would keep his word. She may have known that he'd kept his promise to his dying wife and not remarried.

Had Hemings stayed in France, she probably would have done so only if her brother James also stayed. But she would have been an unmarried mother, and life would have been difficult. She would have had to figure out how to earn money, and she wasn't used to hard work, so her options were limited.

The French Revolution was also beginning, and things were very uncertain in the country. Hemings might have been afraid of the type of future she could expect for herself and her child.

There was also the matter of Jefferson's influence over her. He was a master of words, and in addition to any promise

This painting by George Fuller is called *The Quadroon*. There are no portraits of Sally Hemings, but this one suggests what she may have looked like, since she was just one-quarter black, like the woman portrayed.

about her future children's freedom, he might have made other guarantees that finally persuaded her to return to America. The lives of Hemings's children suggest that she might have swayed Jefferson to give them certain privileges if she returned to the United States.

According to Madison Hemings's account, his mother had a "treaty" with Jefferson in which he promised to set her children free when they became of age. In exchange, Sally had to return to America—and slavery. At first, "she refused to return with him." But Jefferson "promised her extraordinary privileges" including "a solemn pledge" to free her children when they turned twenty-one years old.[1]

Jumping the Broom

Enslaved men and women didn't enjoy the same type of wedding celebrations that whites did. The nature of their enslavement prevented slaves from having legal marriages. Instead, black couples "jumped the broom." For enslaved people, the ceremony came the closest they could to a recognized union. They jumped the broom in front of witnesses, so everyone knew they were together.

Neither the law nor the slaveholder recognized the "marriage" as a legal contract. Still, it was a time for celebration when couples had these ceremonies. Other enslaved people on the plantation—and in some cases, slaves from nearby plantations—took part. A lucky bride would have been given time to make a nice dress, or perhaps her mistress provided her with a hand-me-down. Some owners provided food. A broomstick lay on the ground, and the couple literally jumped over it, either one at a time or together. This simple act joined them in marriage, even if the state did not acknowledge it.

Sally's initial refusal to return to Virginia suggests that she knew she could live as a free woman. Paris meant freedom for her and any children of hers. It also meant that she could marry a white man if she wanted.

Unlike the one-drop rule in America, which gave a racial status of black to anyone with any African ancestry, no matter how white they appeared, France's one-drop rule functioned in the opposite manner: "People who had any European ancestry were allowed to marry white partners without restriction."[2] So had Hemings stayed in France, her choice of potential husbands was legally wider than it was in America.

In the United States, the government didn't recognize a union between slaves as legal and binding. Enslaved couples didn't marry in a church; they often just "jumped the broom," and this simple act recognized their marriage. Few slaveholders recorded these unions, although they may have recorded the births of the couple's children. They did this more as a way of keeping track of "property" and less as a celebration of family.

By not keeping records of slave marriages, perhaps owners didn't find it as hard to sell family members away from each other.

Up from Slavery

Hemings's children, like all of the Hemingses, seemed to enjoy privileges that other enslaved people didn't. Her sons grew up learning to play instruments, including the violin (just as Jefferson had), and learned the carpentry trade. Harriet Hemings learned textile weaving and spinning, although she didn't grow up having to earn a living this way. Instead, by giving the Hemings's children mostly light chores, it seems Jefferson prepared them for adult roles that were less connected to the hard life of field slaves and more in line with tradespeople. He expected Harriet to "be a successful wife and mother, which is exactly what she turned out to be." He clearly didn't imagine a life for her as a typical slave woman; her mother hadn't experienced that type of life, either. As for the boys, he saw that they were "trained to be the types of workers he admired the most—carpenters and joiners, instead of blacksmiths, gardeners, or hostlers."[3]

It appears that Jefferson kept his promise to Hemings. Beverley "ran away" at age twenty-three instead of twenty-one, but Harriet was twenty-one when she left Monticello. Scholars believe Beverley waited two years before leaving so that Harriet could join him soon after his departure.

Jefferson's will granted manumission to Madison and Eston and allowed them to continue living in Virginia, close to their mother and family members.

During his lifetime, Jefferson sold a fair number of enslaved people. Why he didn't sell more (to settle his debt) is unknown. It seems odd that Jefferson never chose the obvious solution to his financial problems. Instead, he allowed Beverley and Harriet to leave Monticello, even playing a secondhand role in Harriet's departure by giving money to his overseer, Edmund Bacon, to give to her. This didn't help his debt situation.

The Thomas Jefferson Foundation has worked to expand education about slave life at Monticello, including compiling oral histories from the descendants of the plantation's slaves.

Jefferson had already shown that he was a man of his word by not remarrying after his wife's death. The freedom of Sally Hemings's children also indicates that he kept his promises. But why didn't he free her?

We won't ever know Jefferson's exact reasons for not granting freedom to Sally Hemings. In fact, he only freed one female slave, and that was Harriet Hemings, her daughter.

Maybe he considered the idea of freeing Sally, especially around the time when Callender's stories first made their rounds. But remember that while Callender's accusations were the most public, community members had long whispered about Jefferson's involvement with Hemings. Their entanglement wasn't news to Virginia planter society. Jefferson ultimately continued to enslave Hemings and her children—until they reached adulthood.

Some historians have raised the idea that Jefferson and Hemings had more than a master-slave relationship and suggest that he did not free her because he wanted her to remain at Monticello. He could not have legally wed her because Virginia did not allow interracial marriages. Instead, over their thirty-eight-year association, Hemings lacked the legal protections that having the status of wife would have given her. Maybe she took comfort in the few promises Jefferson made to her. She couldn't be free, but her children would lead different lives.

The 1782 manumission law may have prevented Jefferson from granting Hemings her freedom in his will also. When Jefferson died in 1826, Hemings was fifty-three years old. The law didn't allow for the manumission of slaves over the age of forty-five unless a slaveholder provided support for them. Lawmakers put this age limit in place to prevent owners from abandoning elderly slaves who had no way of supporting themselves. Although Jefferson's will didn't grant Hemings freedom, his daughter, Martha, gave her "her time."

THE CONTROVERSY CONTINUES

Nearly two centuries after their deaths, the relationship between Thomas Jefferson and Sally Hemings bears examination. There tend to be three groups of opinion about the matter. The first group maintains that Jefferson didn't father any of Hemings's children. The second says that he probably fathered at least one, and maybe all, of her children. The last group is unsure but awaits evidence to form a conclusion.

Why do people have such strong opinions about Jefferson and Hemings? Those who deny all evidence that Jefferson fathered Hemings's children have been particularly outspoken about the issue. The skeptics include Jefferson's own family members.

The Skeptics

Martha Jefferson Randolph, Jefferson's daughter, wanted very much to protect her father's reputation, even after his death. Perhaps the Jeffersons didn't talk about the supposed relationship between Jefferson and Hemings outside of the family, but it seems they did inside of it. Martha Randolph went so far as to

United in Death

After the friendship between Jefferson and John Adams nearly ended around 1800, the two men didn't speak or exchange letters for over a decade. Adams finally reached out to his old friend in 1812. They resumed their friendship and remained in touch over the next several years.

Was it just a strange coincidence that they died on the same day? It was July 4, 1826, fifty years after the signing of the Declaration of Independence. Adams was ninety years old and dying. As America celebrated the anniversary of its independence from Great Britain, Adams remarked that Jefferson still lived. But this wasn't true. Adams didn't know that several hours before, Jefferson had died.

His old friend (and one-time enemy) had passed away surrounded by family and friends. Two of the men who were so important to the founding of the United States died within hours of each other.

tell her children they had a duty to defend their grandfather's reputation. She was the same daughter who claimed that Jefferson hadn't been at Monticello for fifteen months before the birth of one of Hemings's children. Obviously, Randolph did this (despite it being untrue) as a way to deny her father's involvement with Hemings.

In fact, careful examination of records shows that Jefferson was at Monticello nine months before the birth of *all* of Hemings's children. Before he retired from politics, he was away from home a great deal. And certainly other men around Monticello, both enslaved and white, could have potentially fathered her offspring. But it's no coincidence that Hemings "never became pregnant when Jefferson was away from home."[1]

Desperate to protect the politician from scandal, however, the Jeffersons even named other men as possible fathers of Hemings's offspring. Two of the men, Peter and Samuel Carr, were Jefferson's nephews. The family explained that Hemings's children looked like Jefferson because his nephews looked like him, too. Depending on who told the story, either brother could be responsible.

The Jeffersons also argued that no one saw Hemings and the politician sneaking around together. The family maintained that someone would have seen her leaving Jefferson's sleeping quarters at some point. This stands out as one of the weaker arguments. If Jefferson wanted to be private about his sexual relationship with Hemings, he would have made sure no one saw them engaged in this way. We don't know how much time Hemings and Jefferson spent together alone. It's hard to say whether they had private moments once a month or just once a year.

And above all, Jefferson valued his privacy.

Close examination of the bedrooms at Monticello point to just how possible it was for Jefferson and Hemings to spend time together without anyone knowing. The design of the house gives visitors a sense of openness and visibility. However, the actual layout allows for a lot of privacy. This is especially true for Jefferson's personal rooms. His grandson, Thomas Jefferson Randolph, said he never saw or heard even the tiniest hint of improper behavior. This isn't surprising given the sleeping arrangements.

Jefferson's sleeping quarters were far away from the rest of the house, including everyone else's bedrooms. He guarded his privacy well, even from his daughters. His library, sleeping area, and study were all private areas. However, one person at Monticello—Sally Hemings—could go to and from these rooms. Jefferson's family members did not know Jefferson's

In 2012, a new outdoor exhibit opened at Monticello. Called *Landscape of Slavery: Mulberry Row at Monticello*, the exhibit offers insight into how life was for the many slaves there.

personal quarters had private entrances. His bedroom was well hidden from view and "equipped with at least two entrances: a 'front door' off the entrance hall and a back passage from the library and study."[2] In addition, Jefferson added more entrances to his bedroom, and at least one connected to passages that led to the slave quarters where Hemings lived.

Although he frequently entertained guests at Monticello, Jefferson also loved his privacy.

Some of the people who remain skeptical that a Jefferson-Hemings relationship took place have also ignored the black people who've weighed in on the topic. These African Americans included slaves, former slaves, and free people of color. Black people could not testify in court during slavery, and this often stopped their stories, no matter how truthful, from coming to light.

Several days after Madison Hemings's 1873 interview appeared, the editor of a rival newspaper published an argument against his claims. Editor John A. Jones said that black people had a habit of claiming white people as their ancestors in an effort to "better" themselves. In short, Jones suggested that Madison Hemings only named Jefferson as his father to appear more respectable than he actually was.[3]

Some months later, the *Pike County Republican* printed an interview with former Monticello slave Israel Jefferson in agreement with Madison Hemings's account.[4] This led to objections from Jefferson's grandson Thomas Jefferson Randolph. He accused the slaves of jealousy. According to him, envy motivated them to single out Thomas Jefferson as the father. He said other slaves refused to believe that the Hemingses could be as intelligent and trustworthy as they were on their own. Apparently, they needed a white ancestor to have these traits.

But Israel Jefferson simply agreed with Madison Hemings. That doesn't suggest jealousy. And the fair-skinned appearance of the Hemingses made it quite clear that they had white ancestors.

Enslaved blacks, much like their African ancestors, relied heavily on the oral tradition. Forbidden by law to read and write, they passed along family stories and history by word of mouth. Whites may have refused to believe the stories of blacks, but it turns out that much of "the oral testimony among the slaves is turning out to be rather accurate."[5] This isn't surprising. Who spent more time among white families than the people who cared for their homes, their farms, and their children? In most cases, white men and women talked about private and public matters in the company of their slaves, almost as if their slaves didn't exist or lacked thoughts and feelings similar to their own. Enslaved

men and women heard plenty of gossip, rumors, truths, and lies. They mostly exchanged what they heard with one another.

If anyone noticed the comings and goings of Jefferson and Hemings, it was much more likely to be the people who worked on the plantation.

Cosway and DNA

In Paris, Jefferson met Maria Cosway. The twenty-seven-year-old must have seemed a beautiful vision to him with her

96

Troy Harding, right, is one of Sally Hemings's descendants through her son, Madison. Madison was the only one of her children not to pass for white after leaving Monticello.

"luminous blue eyes, exquisite skin, and a halo of golden curls."[6] When they met, Jefferson was recently widowed. He also had two young daughters to raise. Most men in his predicament chose to remarry so that their children would have a motherly influence in their lives. Due to Jefferson's promise to his dying wife, however, remarrying was out of the question.

Maria Cosway met Thomas Jefferson in France. Although married, she exchanged affectionate letters with Jefferson, but she returned to England with her husband, leaving Jefferson despondent.

If he'd wanted to marry Maria Cosway, he couldn't have. She already had a husband. Still, Jefferson found her enchanting.

Historians who doubt Jefferson fathered Hemings's children point out how much Jefferson seemed to love Cosway. Why would Jefferson choose a teenaged girl who wasn't in the same social class as he was over a woman who was? Especially since Cosway seemed unhappily married, and she and Jefferson spent time alone together. They also exchanged long letters that hinted at shared feelings.

After Cosway left Paris, Jefferson wrote the love letter known as "My Head and My Heart." At more than four thousand words, this extremely long letter displays his "great wretchedness of spirit" and his "considerable physical pain" at being separated from Cosway.[7] Despite his strong emotional attachment to her, no proof exists that Jefferson and Cosway did anything more than exchange affectionate letters and notes.

Man of Letters

Jefferson wrote an enormous amount of letters during his life. He also collected an extraordinary number. He kept around twenty-five thousand letters from friends and family members. Jefferson also made copies of his own letters, and of those, he had about eighteen thousand. He organized them into a journal dated from the years 1783 to 1826.

The journal contains more than 650 pages. Curiously, no letters to his mother and wife factor into these figures. Historians have asserted that letters to and from these two women, who were so important to him, could have told us so much more about him. Just knowing why he destroyed these letters could provide more clues about the real Jefferson.

Mulberry Row is where some of the slaves at Monticello lived, including Sally Hemings. These quarters were reserved for slaves who worked in the plantation house and not in the fields.

Examining his feelings for Cosway, Jefferson's defenders point out that he wasn't attracted to dark skin and African features. But how many of these features did Sally Hemings have? She was very fair skinned and had long hair that fell down her back. These sound like the very traits that Jefferson would find acceptable.

Others simply believe that Jefferson was too honorable a man to have fathered Hemings's children. After all, he was a Founding Father. He wrote much of the Declaration of Independence. He negotiated treaties, furthered American causes, and greatly increased the size of the United States. To these people, Jefferson represents more than just a man. He represents a moral compass, an institution. They refuse to think of him as a human man, with very human failings and weaknesses.

They want to believe that he remained completely devoted to his late wife. They refuse to entertain the idea that Jefferson had romantic feelings about another woman, much less had sexual relations with one. Perhaps if Jefferson hadn't been so important and influential, his defenders might be more willing to accept the idea of a connection with Hemings. But, to them, "Jefferson represents much more, for the Jefferson legacy

> *In his love letter to Maria Cosway, Jefferson reveals his "physical pain" at their separation.*

is...linked to the formation of the American republic and, more generally, to the American national character."[8] Just the thought of Jefferson being involved with Hemings makes them question the very character of the nation.

A 1998 DNA test muted much of the debate between the Jefferson-Randolph family members and Hemings descendants. The genetic study linked descendants of Eston Hemings to a male in the Jefferson line. The British science journal *Nature* published the results. While Dr. Eugene Foster and other researchers established that a "Jefferson male" fathered Eston, the study couldn't prove which Jefferson male did.

As soon as the news broke, Jefferson defenders quickly pointed out that the evidence couldn't definitively prove Thomas Jefferson fathered Sally Hemings's children. He was but one of the possible fathers. In addition, the results only included Eston Hemings's descendants, not all of Sally Hemings's children.

The genetic study did rule out the Carr brothers as fathers, a major blow to the Jefferson defenders. It disproved the stories some Jeffersons told about the paternity of Sally Hemings's children. But the findings still left other Jefferson males, such as his brother, Randolph, as possible fathers.

The president's defenders have been quick to name any other Jefferson male as the father of Hemings's children. In their efforts to paint Jefferson as a lifelong grieving husband, devoted father, and honorable man, they have no qualms about damaging Sally Hemings's reputation. What does linking her to any man they could place at Monticello imply about her values?

When biographers like Dumas Malone argue that they find it unthinkable that Jefferson could have taken advantage of Hemings, they ignore that influential men routinely used women in the lower social classes for sexual gratification. During the context in which Jefferson and Hemings lived, that type of relationship between slaveholder and enslaved wasn't at all unusual.

Once the DNA results established a link between a Jefferson male and Eston Hemings, another question followed. Did this man father all of her children? Considering their appearance—more European than African—it's probable that all of the children had a white father. Why not Thomas Jefferson?

If Hemings's children had different fathers, she probably had no control over the matter.

In many cases, an enslaved woman may have been "married" or partnered off to an enslaved man. Also, if her slaveholder sold her, she may have then been partnered with another enslaved man on a new plantation. Because they had no legal rights—to their own bodies or their children—female slaves often had children with more than one man.

In Hemings's case, it's likely that Jefferson fathered all of her children. The timelines match up, and Jefferson gave all of her children special privileges. Moreover, he never identified the father of any of her children in his farm book. Given this, Hemings's children were almost certainly Jefferson's as well.

THEIR LEGACY

It's clear that race, class, and gender defined the interactions between Thomas Jefferson and Sally Hemings, but one must also consider these factors when examining the public's reaction to the pair. Would Jefferson defenders have an easier time accepting that the president fathered Hemings's children had she been free and white rather than mixed-race and enslaved?

The concerns that affected the lives of whites and blacks centuries ago still exist today. Although interracial marriage is now legal, some people still don't like or accept the idea of people of different races being together and having children. But interracial pairings have taken place since America's colonial days. In fact, it's one of the characteristics that helped shape the nation. The United States is known as a "melting pot" precisely because of the large number of cultures and colors that make up the country.

Recognizing Hemings's Descendants

After the publication of the 1998 DNA results, the Monticello Association, made up of Jefferson descendants, decided to conduct its own research about the Jefferson-Hemings link. Members wanted to know if the 1998 research findings were accurate.

> *The Thomas Jefferson Foundation now believes there's a strong likelihood that Thomas Jefferson and Sally Hemings had children together.*

In 2000, the research committee announced that there was a "strong likelihood" that Jefferson and Hemings had a relationship that produced at least one child and possibly all of her children.[1] They made it clear that a relationship between the two couldn't be definitively proven but made their evaluation based on the best evidence available.

In 2002, however, the Monticello Association dealt Hemings's descendants a blow. Because no committee could prove without a doubt that Thomas Jefferson fathered Hemings's children, the association voted against admitting Hemings's descendants into the association. Did Hemings's race and class factor into the association's decision. It may have. By refusing to grant admission to her descendants, the Monticello Association essentially continued to regard her descendants as "illegitimate."

Also, the association is more than just a gathering of Jefferson's descendants. It also owns and manages the Monticello cemetery, the gravesite where descendants of Jefferson and his wife, Martha, are buried. When the association voted not to let in Hemings's family members, it prevented them from being buried in the graveyard. It seems that in life and death, the association voted them out.

But in 2012, the Thomas Jefferson Foundation announced that it now believes that Jefferson fathered

While Thomas Jefferson, many of his descendants, and his wife, Martha, are buried at Monticello, Hemings's descendants are not buried in the Jefferson family cemetery.

Sally Hemings's children. This marked a shift from the foundation's earlier view. The change in perspective lines up with what many historians currently believe about the Hemings-Jefferson connection.

What is the legacy of Jefferson and Hemings today?

Their descendants include people who identify as black, white, and mixed race. Some of them look white, but identify as black. Even though the Hemings clan can't currently claim membership in the Monticello Association, many of them have met with Thomas and Martha Jefferson's descendants. A number of them accept each other as family, despite the differences in their backgrounds.

By acknowledging their relatives and distant relatives across class and race lines, they're doing what many Americans do every day. The book *Jefferson's Children: The Story of One American Family* includes the stories of people from both sides

Family Reunion

Some of Thomas and Martha Jefferson's descendants warmly accepted Sally Hemings's descendants as family. Others haven't been quite as open. Not surprisingly, some of Hemings's family members feel offended that they have to "prove" they're related to Jefferson.

The different branches of these families have a lot of emotions about the whole Jefferson-Hemings story. Some may feel proud, while others may feel shame. Discovering their ancestry, be it the white part or the black part, proved to be a shock for many of the descendants. Even so, most feel a sense of connection to their newfound family members.

Descendants of Jefferson and Hemings have met at reunions. During these meetings, they have taken group photos that show just how diverse the family members are.

of the family. They talk about their family histories and how they feel about the Jefferson-Hemings story. Some believe the two had a relationship, while others do not. Some of them can easily trace their ancestry back (particularly the ones in the Thomas and Martha Jefferson line), and others have to rely more on oral tradition.

Until the 1998 DNA study, many Hemings descendants had no idea the mixed-race, enslaved woman was their ancestor. The research did more than establish a connection between the Jeffersons and the Hemingses. For many descendants, it shed light into the past. Since the DNA study, many of them have met each other at Monticello events and reunions.

What Is Black or White in America?

During the slavery era, being identified as a certain race usually had serious lifelong consequences. To be black often meant living in slavery and not being recognized as human. Instead, slaveholders treated blacks as property, or human chattel. They bought and sold slaves, and in many cases, broke up families by selling parents away from their children and sisters away from brothers.

To be white, however, offered a completely different way of life. This meant freedom. With this freedom came many opportunities that even free black people didn't have.

Is it any surprise, then, that some black people who had "white" features chose to pass into white communities? By doing so, they tried to give themselves better lives. This included education and paying jobs. Knowing how to read and write opened up possibilities that enslaved people didn't have. They also avoided terrible treatment at the hands of slaveholders.

People who passed sacrificed a great deal when they "crossed the color line." In most cases, "passing" resulted in leaving

White, Black, Other

Race can change, at least on paper. After Hemings became unofficially free, she lived with her sons Madison and Eston in Charlottesville, Virginia. An 1830 census lists all three of them as free white people. Just a few years later, in a special census, Hemings called herself a mulatto.

The 1833 special census counted the number of free black people in the area who might want to resettle in Africa. The Hemingses, of course, stayed in America. Some branched out from Virginia into Ohio and Wisconsin. They made new lives for themselves as free black, or white, people. By continuing the rich oral history of their ancestors, they made sure Sally Hemings's name wasn't forgotten.

behind their black relatives and cutting off contact with them. Why? Imagine living as a white person in an area where all of your neighbors are white. You're only able to be free and have a job because people believe you're something you're not. If your black relatives showed up at your home, how would you explain who they were without giving yourself away? Do you believe these neighbors would be kind and understanding during a time when people believed whites and blacks should live separately?

So, people who passed into white society often did so completely. They married white people and had "white" children. Eventually, some of Hemings's descendants came to look as if they had no black ancestors at all. They considered themselves to be white people and lived that way.

But what is it to be white? Or black? Is it all about skin color, hair texture, and facial features? Genetics is complicated, and biracial children can look any number of ways. Sometimes one biracial child appears to have a different racial background from other children in the same family. Under Virginia law, Hemings's children were considered white because they had much more European ancestry than African ancestry. But because Hemings was an enslaved woman, the law made them slaves as well.

Even so, Virginia's racial classification system wasn't as complicated as other states, like Louisiana. It also wasn't as complex as the system throughout much of the Caribbean. There, someone who is called black in America may be Creole, high Creole, or something else entirely.

The American "one-drop rule" that defined anyone with a drop of black blood as black didn't make a lot of sense. No one can have "one drop" of any type of blood. That's not how genetics works. The concept was simply another way for white people to prevent black people from taking a more active part in society. It also created more slaves, which helped the US economy. Labeling mixed-race people as white would have meant less slave labor. Capitalism drove this nonsensical rule about race.

Does race still matter today? While many people dream of a colorblind society, others still use race or color as a reason to dislike someone else. Racial discrimination is easy to carry out if you look at someone and recognize the individual as white, black, etc. But what if the person isn't easy to categorize? Some of Hemings's descendants looked like and lived as white people, but were they really? Not everyone who "looks white" actually identifies that way, and the same is true for some "black" people.

Nearly two centuries after their deaths, the story of Jefferson and Hemings continues to invite questions and controversy. Historians and scholars seem to find out something new about Jefferson all the time. The sheer number of books about him

This portrait of Thomas Jefferson by Gilbert Stuart shows the president later in life.

shows how much interest still exists. Literature on Hemings isn't as extensive, but many people remain fascinated by her. Because we have no letters between the two, and because Jefferson didn't make more than the typical plantation owner's notes about her, we don't know how he actually felt about her. The mystery of their connection has led to endless speculation.

We can only rely on the evidence we do have about their interactions. DNA is one of the strongest pieces of evidence we have about their link. And the notes, records, and oral history that remain forever join Thomas Jefferson and Sally Hemings together in history.

1743

Thomas Jefferson is born.

1757

Jefferson's father, Peter, dies.

1760

Jefferson attends the College of William and Mary.

1767

Jefferson begins practicing law.

1768

Construction on Monticello begins.

1769

Jefferson is elected to the Virginia House of Burgesses.

1770

Jefferson argues his first "freedom suit."

1772

Jefferson marries Martha Wayles Skelton.

1773

Sally Hemings is born; John Wayles dies, and his daughter Martha inherits her father's slaves, including Hemings.

The Boston Tea Party takes place.

1774

Jefferson retires from his law practice.

1775

Hemings comes to live at Monticello.

The war between the colonies and Britain begins.

1776

The Declaration of Independence is signed.

Jefferson's mother, Jane, dies.

1779

Jefferson is elected Virginia governor.

1780

He wins reelection.

1781

Jefferson retires as war governor of Virginia during the American Revolution.

1782

Martha Jefferson dies.

1783

The Revolutionary War ends; Jefferson is elected to the Continental Congress.

1784

Jefferson goes to Paris; his youngest daughter, Lucy, dies.

1785

Thomas Jefferson is appointed American minister to France.

1785

Jefferson publishes *Notes on the State of Virginia*.

1787

Hemings arrives in Europe with Polly Jefferson.

1789

Jefferson is named secretary of state.

1790

Hemings has her first child.

1796

Jefferson is elected vice president to President John Adams.

1800

Jefferson is elected US president.

1802

The *Richmond Recorder* publishes an article accusing Jefferson of having an affair with Hemings.

1803

Jefferson negotiates the Louisiana Purchase.

1804

Jefferson is reelected president.

1809

Jefferson retires to Monticello.

1822

Beverley and Harriet Hemings "run away."

1826

Thomas Jefferson dies.

1827

Hemings is given "her time."

1835

Sally Hemings dies.

CHAPTER 1
Public Servant, Private Citizen

1. Virginia Scharff, *The Women Jefferson Loved* (New York, NY: Harper, 2010), p. 47.
2. Russell Roberts, *The Life and Times of Thomas Jefferson* (Newark, DE: Mitchell Lane Publishers, 2007), p. 19.

CHAPTER 2
Kept Woman

1. Julian Boyd, *The Papers of Thomas Jefferson*, vol. XI (Princeton, NJ: Princeton University Press, 1950), p. 503.
2. James A. Bear, ed., *Jefferson at Monticello* (Charlottesville, VA: University Press of Virginia, 1967), p. 4.
3. Fawn M. Brodie, *Thomas Jefferson, an Intimate History* (New York, NY: W.W. Norton, 1974), p. 216.
4. Ibid.
5. Madison Hemings, "Life Among the Lowly, No. 1," *Pike County (Ohio) Republican*, March 13, 1873.

CHAPTER 3
The Trip to Paris

1. Fawn M. Brodie, *Thomas Jefferson, an Intimate History* (New York, NY: W.W. Norton, 1974), p. 217.
2. Julian Boyd, *The Papers of Thomas Jefferson*, vol. VIII (Princeton, NJ: Princeton University Press, 1950), p. 404.

CHAPTER 4
The Controversy Then

1. Clarence E. Walker, *Mongrel Nation: The America Begotten by Thomas Jefferson and Sally Hemings* (Charlottesville, VA: University of Virginia Press, 2009), p. 21.
2. Henry Wiencek, *Master of the Mountain: Thomas Jefferson and His Slaves* (New York, NY: Farrar, Straus and Giroux, 2012), p. 46.
3. Ibid., p. 47.
4. Lucia Stanton, *Slavery at Monticello* (Charlottesville, VA: Thomas Jefferson Memorial Foundation, 1993), p. 34.
5. Jan Ellen Lewis and Peter S. Onuf, eds., *Sally Hemings & Thomas Jefferson: History, Memory, and Civic Culture* (Charlottesville, VA: University of Virginia Press, 1999), p. 189.

CHAPTER 5
All of Hemings's Children

1. Madison Hemings, "Life Among the Lowly, No. 1," *Pike County (Ohio) Republican*, March 13, 1873.
2. Annette Gordon-Reed, *The Hemingses of Monticello: An American Family* (New York, NY: W.W. Norton, 2008), p. 602.
3. *Daily Scioto Gazette*, August 1, 1902.
4. Annette Gordon-Reed, *Thomas Jefferson and Sally Hemings: An American Controversy* (Charlottesville, VA: University Press of Virginia, 1997), p. 54.

CHAPTER 6
Sally's Sacrifice

1. Madison Hemings, "Life Among the Lowly, No. 1," *Pike County (Ohio) Republican*, March 13, 1873.
2. Annette Gordon-Reed, *The Hemingses of Monticello: An American Family* (New York, NY: W.W. Norton, 2008), p. 350.
3. Ibid., p. 598.

CHAPTER 7
The Controversy Continues

1. Andrew Burstein, *Jefferson's Secrets: Death and Desire at Monticello* (New York, NY: Basic Books, 2005), p. 114.
2. Alan Pell Crawford, *Twilight at Monticello: The Final Years of Thomas Jefferson* (New York, NY: Random House, 2008), p. 144.
3. "Reply of Waverly Watchman editor, John A. Jones, dated March 18, 1873," PBS.org, accessed January 9, 2018, http://www.pbs.org/wgbh/pages/frontline/shows/jefferson/cron/1873rebuttal.html.
4. Clarence E. Walker, *Mongrel Nation: The America Begotten by Thomas Jefferson and Sally Hemings* (Charlottesville, VA: University of Virginia Press, 2009), p. 81.
5. Jan Ellen Lewis and Peter S. Onuf, eds., *Sally Hemings & Thomas Jefferson: History, Memory, and Civic Culture* (Charlottesville, VA: University of Virginia Press, 1999), p. 146.
6. Fawn M. Brodie, *Thomas Jefferson, an Intimate History* (New York, NY: W.W. Norton, 1974), p. 200.
7. Ibid., p. 210.
8. Walker, p. 27.

CHAPTER 8
Their Legacy

1. "Appendix H: Sally Hemings and Her Children: Report of the Research Committee on Thomas Jefferson and Sally Hemings," Thomas Jefferson Foundation, February 2002, https://www.monticello.org/site/plantation-and-slavery/appendix-h-sally-hemings-and-her-children.

abolitionist Any activist who fought to end the transatlantic slave trade during the 1800s.

alliance When two or more people, countries, businesses, or other entities enter into an agreement about a matter; an organization whose members share common interests.

apprenticeship The act of learning an occupation or trade under an expert in the field

classism Showing favor to one social class over another.

colonist A person who settles in a land or territory while remaining a citizen of another country, or a "parent" country.

concubine A woman, often of a lower social status, kept by a man for a sexual relationship.

enslaved The condition of being a slave.

heir Someone who legally inherits property, money, or titles from another person.

industriousness Being active and busy.

interracial Involving people of two different races.

intimate Close and affectionate; sexual in nature.

manumission The act of a slaveholder freeing an enslaved person.

miscegenation The mixing of two races of people, often used to describe the racial mix of white and non-white people.

mulatto A person with one black parent and one white parent. Today the term is considered offensive and biracial is used instead.

offspring A child (or children) of someone.

partus doctrine Law that said children inherited the status of their mother, whether enslaved or free.

sentimental Emotional; involving the feelings.

shadow family A family kept separate from a man's legal wife and children.

sobriety Not being drunk or intoxicated, especially for a period of time.

BOOKS

Bradley, Kimberly Brubaker. *Jefferson's Sons: A Founding Father's Secret Children*. London, UK: Puffin Books, 2013.

Kennedy, Alexander. *Thomas Jefferson: The Blood of Patriots*. Seattle, WA: Amazon Digital Services, 2016.

Meacham, John. *Thomas Jefferson: President and Philosopher*. New York, NY: Crown Books for Young Readers, 2014.

Oachs, Emily Rose. *Thomas Jefferson's Presidency*. Minneapolis, MN: Lerner Publications, 2016.

WEBSITES

Frontline: The History of a Secret
https://www.pbs.org/wgbh/pages/frontline/shows/jefferson/cron/
Chronological account of rumors about Jefferson and Hemings and evidence of the relationship.

**Thomas Jefferson and Sally Hemings:
A Brief Account**
https://www.monticello.org/site/plantation-and-slavery/thomas-jefferson-
and-sally-hemings-brief-account
Brief account given by the Thomas Jefferson Foundation on the supposed nature of Jefferson's relationship with Hemings.

FILMS

Thomas Jefferson: A Film by Ken Burns (1997)
Jefferson in Paris (1995)